THE 30-MINUTE SHAKESPEARE
HAMLET

"Nick Newlin's work as a teaching artist for Folger Education during the past thirteen years has provided students, regardless of their experience with Shakespeare or being on stage, a unique opportunity to tread the boards at the Folger Theatre. Working with students to edit Shakespeare's plays for performance at the annual Folger Shakespeare Festivals has enabled students to gain new insights into the Bard's plays, build their skills of comprehension and critical reading, and just plain have fun working collaboratively with their peers.

Folger Education promotes performance-based teaching of Shakespeare's plays, providing students with an interactive approach to Shakespeare's plays in which they participate in a close reading of the text through intellectual, physical, and vocal engagement. Newlin's *The 30-Minute Shakespeare* series is an invaluable resource for teachers of Shakespeare, and for all who are interested in performing the plays."

ROBERT YOUNG, PH.D.
DIRECTOR OF EDUCATION
FOLGER SHAKESPEARE LIBRARY

Hamlet: The 30-Minute Shakespeare
ISBN 978-1-935550-24-2
Adaptation, essays, and notes © 2010 by Nick Newlin

Cover design by Sarah Juckniess
Printed in the United States of America

Distributed by Consortium Book Sales & Distribution
www.cbsd.com

NICOLO WHIMSEY PRESS
www.30MinuteShakespeare.com

Art Director: Sarah Juckniess
Managing Editors: Katherine Little, Leah Gordon

THE TRAGICALL HISTORIE

of

HAMLET

PRINCE OF DENMARKE

THE 30-MINUTE SHAKESPEARE

Written by **WILLIAM SHAKESPEARE**

Abridged AND Edited

by **NICK NEWLIN**

Nicolo Whimsey
Press

Brandywine, MD

To the students,
faculty, and staff
at Benjamin Banneker
Academic High School
in Washington, D.C.

for bringing life
to Shakespeare

Special thanks to Joanne Flynn, Bill Newlin, Eliza Newlin Carney, William and Louisa Newlin, Michael Tolaydo, Hilary Kacser, Sarah Juckniess, Katherine Little, Eva Zimmerman, Leah Gordon, Julie Schaper and all of Consortium, Leo Bowman and the students, faculty, and staff at Banneker Academic High School, and Robert Young Ph.D., and the Folger Shakespeare Library, especially the wonderful Education Department.

✳ TABLE OF CONTENTS

✳ NO EXPERIENCE NECESSARY

I was not a big "actor type" in high school, so if you weren't either, or if the young people you work with are not, then this book is for you. Whether or not you work with "actor types," you can use this book to stage a lively and captivating thirty-minute version of a Shakespeare play. No experience is necessary.

When I was about eleven years old, my parents took me to see Shakespeare's *Two Gentlemen of Verona*, which was being performed as a Broadway musical. I didn't comprehend every word I heard, but I was enthralled with the language, the characters, and the story, and I understood enough of it to follow along. From then on, I associated Shakespeare with *fun*.

Of course Shakespeare is fun. The Elizabethan audiences knew it, which is one reason he was so popular. It didn't matter that some of the language eluded them. The characters were passionate and vibrant, and their conflicts were compelling. Young people study Shakespeare in high school, but more often than not they read his work like a text book and then get quizzed on academic elements of the play, such as plot, theme, and vocabulary. These are all very interesting, but not nearly as interesting as standing up and performing a scene! It is through performance that the play comes alive and all its "academic" elements are revealed. There is nothing more satisfying to a student or teacher than the feeling of "owning" a Shakespeare play, and that can only come from performing it.

But Shakespeare's plays are often two or more hours long, making the performance of an entire play almost out of the question. One can perform a single scene, which is certainly a good start, but what about the story? What about the changes a character goes through as the play progresses? When school groups perform one scene unedited, or when they lump several plays together, the audience can get lost. This is why I have always preferred to tell the story of the play.

The 30-Minute Shakespeare gives students and teachers a chance to get up on their feet and act out a Shakespeare play in half an hour, using his language. The emphasis is on key scenes, with narrative bridges between scenes to keep the audience caught up on the action. The stage directions are built into this script so that young actors do not have to stand in one place; they can move and tell the story with their actions as well as their words. And it can all be done in a classroom during class time!

That is where this book was born: not in a research library, a graduate school lecture, a professional stage, or even an after-school drama club. All of the play cuttings in *The 30-Minute Shakespeare* were first rehearsed in a D.C. public high school English class, and performed successfully at the Folger Shakespeare Library's annual Secondary School Shakespeare Festival. The players were not necessarily "actor types." For many of them, this was their first performance in a play.

Something almost miraculous happens when students perform Shakespeare. They "get" it. By occupying the characters and speaking the words out loud, students gain a level of understanding and appreciation that is unachievable by simply reading the text. That is the magic of a performance-based method of learning Shakespeare, and this book makes the formerly daunting task of staging a Shakespeare play possible for anybody.

With *The 30-Minute Shakespeare* book series I hope to help teachers and students produce a Shakespeare play in a short amount of time, thus jump-starting the process of discovering the beauty, magic, and fun of the Bard. Plot, theme, and language reveal themselves through the performance of these half-hour play cuttings, and everybody involved receives the priceless gift of "owning" a piece of Shakespeare. The result is an experience that is fun and engaging, and one that we can all carry with us as we play out our own lives on the stages of the world.

NICK NEWLIN
Brandywine, MD
March 2010

CHARACTERS IN THE PLAY

The following is a list of the characters that appear in this cutting of Hamlet.

Twenty-five actors performed in the original production. This number can be increased to about thirty or decreased to about fifteen by having actors share or double roles.

For the full breakdown of characters, see Sample Program.

KING CLAUDIUS: King of Denmark; murders his brother (Hamlet's father) and marries his widow (Queen Gertrude)

HAMLET: Son of the late King Hamlet; nephew to King Claudius

QUEEN GERTRUDE: Queen of Denmark; mother to Hamlet

POLONIUS: Lord Chamberlain; father to Ophelia

OPHELIA: Daughter to Polonius; sister to Laertes

LAERTES: Son to Polonius; brother to Ophelia

HORATIO: Friend to Hamlet; fellow student at Wittenberg

GHOST: Ghost of Hamlet's father, the late King Hamlet

PLAYER KING: Traveling actor performing *The Murder of Gonzago*

PLAYER QUEEN: Traveling actor performing *The Murder of Gonzago*

POISONER: Traveling actor performing *The Murder of Gonzago*

ADDITIONAL PLAYER

OSRIC: A courtier

LORDS

ATTENDANTS

MARCELLUS: A guard

BERNARDO: A guard

NARRATOR

SCENE 1. (ACT I, SCENE II)

Elsinore. A room of state in the castle.

SOUND OPERATOR *plays* Sound Cue #1 ("Ominous music").

Enter **NARRATOR** *from stage rear, coming downstage center.*

NARRATOR
> Hamlet, the Prince of Denmark, is grieving over his father's death. To make matters worse, his uncle Claudius has become king by marrying Hamlet's mother, Queen Gertrude. Then there is the matter of the ghost . . . .

Enter **KING CLAUDIUS, QUEEN GERTRUDE, HAMLET, POLONIUS, LAERTES, LORDS,** *and* **ATTENDANTS** *from stage right.* **KING CLAUDIUS** *stands stage center with* **QUEEN GERTRUDE** *to his right.* **HAMLET** *stands stage right; all others stand stage left.*

KING CLAUDIUS
> Though yet of Hamlet our dear brother's death
> The memory be green, our hearts in grief,
> We with wisest sorrow think on him.
> Together with our sometime sister, now our queen,

KING CLAUDIUS *holds out his hand to* **QUEEN GERTRUDE**. *She takes it, moving toward him.*

> Have we, with mirth in funeral and with dirge in
>   marriage,
> Taken to wife.

KING CLAUDIUS *looks to* QUEEN GERTRUDE *lovingly.* HAMLET *looks away.*

> But now, my cousin Hamlet, and my son,
> How is it that the clouds still hang on you?

HAMLET
> Not so, my lord; I am too much i' the sun.

QUEEN GERTRUDE
> Good Hamlet, cast thy nighted color off,
> Do not for ever with thy vailed lids
> Seek for thy noble father in the dust:
> Thou know'st 'tis common; all that lives must die,
> Passing through nature to eternity.

HAMLET
> Ay, madam, it is common.

KING CLAUDIUS
> 'Tis sweet and commendable in your nature, Hamlet,
> To give these mourning duties to your father:
> But, you must know, your father lost a father;
> That father lost, lost his: but to persever
> In obstinate condolement, 'tis a fault against the dead.
> Come away.

Exit ALL, *except for* HAMLET, *stage left.*

HAMLET *(moves downstage center)*
> O, that this too too solid flesh would melt
> Thaw and resolve itself into a dew!
> How weary, stale, flat and unprofitable,
> Seem to me all the uses of this world!
> That it should come to this!
> But two months dead:

So excellent a king; that was, to this, *(gestures stage
left to indicate* KING CLAUDIUS*)*
Hyperion to a satyr; so loving to my mother
Frailty, thy name is woman!—
Why she, even she—
O, God! A beast, that wants discourse of reason,
Would have mourn'd longer—married with my uncle,
(addresses audience)
My father's brother.
O, most wicked speed, to post
With such dexterity to incestuous sheets!
But break, my heart; for I must hold my tongue.

Enter HORATIO *from stage right.*

HORATIO

Hail to your lordship!

HAMLET *steps toward* HORATIO *and happily gives him a two-handed handshake.*

HAMLET

I am glad to see you well, Horatio.

HORATIO

My lord, I came to see your father's funeral.

HAMLET *(looks upward)*

My father!—Methinks I see my father.

HORATIO

Where, my lord? *(haltingly, taken aback)*

HAMLET

In my mind's eye, Horatio.

HORATIO

> My lord *(pauses)*, I think I saw him yesternight.

HAMLET

> The king my father!
> For God's love, let me hear.

Enter MARCELLUS, BERNARDO, *and* GHOST *to reenact Horatio's tale.*

HORATIO

> Two nights together with those gentlemen,
> Marcellus and Bernardo, on our watch,
> In the dead vast and middle of the night,
> were thus encounter'd. A figure like your father,
> Armed at point exactly,
> Appears before us, and with solemn march
> Goes slow and stately by us:
> It lifted up its head, like as it would speak;
> But even then the morning cock crew loud,
> And at the sound it shrunk in haste away,
> And vanish'd from our sight.

HAMLET

> 'Tis very strange.
> I will watch to-night;
> Perchance 'twill walk again.

HORATIO

> I warrant it will.

HAMLET

> So, fare you well:
> Upon the platform, 'twixt eleven and twelve,
> I'll visit you.

HORATIO
>My duty to your honor.

Exit HORATIO *stage right.*

HAMLET
>My father's spirit in arms! All is not well;
>Foul deeds will rise,
>Though all the earth o'erwhelm them, to men's eyes.

Exit HAMLET *stage right.*

✳ SCENE 2. (ACT I, SCENE IV)

A platform before the castle.

Enter NARRATOR *from stage rear, coming downstage center.*

NARRATOR
> On the watchmen's platform, the ghost of the
> former king, Hamlet's father, appears to give Hamlet
> disturbing news.

Exit NARRATOR *stage left.*

Enter HAMLET *and* HORATIO *from stage right.*

HAMLET
> The air bites shrewdly; it is very cold.

HORATIO
> Look, my lord, it comes!

Enter GHOST *from stage left.*

HAMLET
> Angels and ministers of grace defend us!
> Bring with thee airs from heaven or blasts from hell,
> King, father: O, answer me!

GHOST *beckons* HAMLET.

HORATIO
> It beckons you to go away with it.

HAMLET
> Then I will follow it.

HORATIO
> Do not, my lord.

HAMLET
> My fate cries out,
> I'll follow thee.

Exit GHOST *and* HAM_ET *stage left.*

HORATIO
> Something is rotten in the state of Denmark.

Exit HORATIO *stage left.*

✳ SCENE 3. (ACT I, SCENE V)

Another part of the platform.

Enter GHOST *and* HAMLET *from stage left.*

HAMLET
> Where wilt thou lead me? Speak; I'll go no further.

GHOST
> I am thy father's spirit,
> Doom'd for a certain term to walk the night,
> And for the day confined to fast in fires,
> Till the foul crimes done in my days of nature
> Are burnt and purged away. List, list, O, list!
> If thou didst ever thy dear father love—

HAMLET
> O God!

GHOST
> Revenge his foul and most unnatural murder.

HAMLET
> Murder!

GHOST
> Now, Hamlet, hear:
> Sleeping in my orchard,
> A serpent stung me.

The serpent that did sting thy father's life
Now wears his crown.

HAMLET

O my prophetic soul! My uncle!

GHOST

Ay, that incestuous, that adulterate beast,
Won to his shameful lust
The will of my most seeming-virtuous queen:
Sleeping within my orchard,
Thy uncle stole,
With juice of cursed hebenon in a vial,
And in the porches of my ears did pour
The leperous distilment;
Thus was I, sleeping, by a brother's hand
Of life, of crown, of queen, at once dispatch'd:
O, horrible! Most horrible!
Adieu, adieu! Hamlet, remember me.

Exit GHOST *stage right.*

HAMLET

Remember thee!
Ay, thou poor ghost, while memory holds a seat
In this distracted globe.
O most pernicious woman!
Smiling, damned villain!

Enter HORATIO *from stage left.*

HAMLET

Give me one poor request, Horatio.

HORATIO

What is't, my lord? I will.

HAMLET
> Never make known what you have seen to-night.

HORATIO
> My lord, I will not.

GHOST *(offstage)*
> Swear.

HORATIO
> O day and night, but this is wondrous strange!

GHOST *(offstage)*
> Swear.

HAMLET
> Rest, rest, perturbed spirit! (**BOTH** *swear)*
> Let us go in together;
> And still your fingers on your lips, I pray.
> The time is out of joint: O cursed spite,
> That ever I was born to set it right!

Exit **HAMLET** *and* **HORATIO** *stage left.*

STAGEHANDS *set throne center stage; set chair stage left of throne.*

✳ SCENE 4. (ACT II, SCENE II)

A room in the castle.

Enter NARRATOR *from stage rear, coming downstage center.*

NARRATOR
> A traveling acting troupe arrives at Elsinore; Hamlet decides to have the players act out his father's murder. *(emphatically)* The play's the thing.

Exit NARRATOR *stage right.*

Enter HAMLET *from stage left.*

HAMLET *(gestures toward center stage)*
> I'll have the players
> Play something like the murder of my father
> Before mine uncle: *(sits on throne)*
> I'll observe his looks;
> If he but blench, I know my course. *(pauses;*
> > *looks out at audience)*
> The play's the thing
> Wherein I'll catch the conscience of the king.

✳ SCENE 5. (ACT III, SCENE I)

A room in the castle.

Enter NARRATOR *from stage rear, coming downstage center.*

NARRATOR
> Hamlet and Ophelia, the daughter of King
> Claudius's chief officer Polonius, have recently
> confessed their affection for each other. But when
> Ophelia's father, bound by the king to spy on
> Hamlet, orders Ophelia to return Hamlet's love
> letters, the prince's vicious and unhinged reaction
> upsets her greatly.

Exit NARRATOR *stage right.*

Enter HAMLET *from stage right.*

Enter OPHELIA *from stage left, holding letters.*

OPHELIA
> My lord, I have remembrances of yours,
> That I have longed long to re-deliver;
> I pray you, now receive them.

HAMLET
> No, not I;
> I never gave you aught.

OPHELIA
> My honor'd lord, you know right well you did;

And, with them, words of so sweet breath composed
As made the things more rich: their perfume lost,
Take these again; for to the noble mind
Rich gifts wax poor when givers prove unkind.
There, my lord. *(gives letters to* HAMLET*)*

HAMLET *steps in close to* OPHELIA *and turns toward her.*

HAMLET
I did love you once.

OPHELIA *(takes a step toward* HAMLET*)*
Indeed, my lord, you made me believe so.

HAMLET *(turns away suddenly)*
You should not have believed me; I loved you not.

HAMLET *returns the letters to* OPHELIA.

OPHELIA *(hurt)*
I was the more deceived.

HAMLET *(points at* OPHELIA*; yells)*
Get thee to a nunnery: why wouldst thou be a
breeder of sinners? Or, if thou wilt needs marry,
marry a fool; for wise men know well enough what
monsters you make of them. *(points again)* To a
nunnery, go, and quickly too. Farewell.

HAMLET *begins to exit stage right.*

OPHELIA
O heavenly powers, restore him!

HAMLET *turns around and comes back toward* OPHELIA.

HAMLET

> God has given you one face, and you make
> yourselves another. Go to, I'll no more on't; it
> hath made me mad. I say, we will have no more
> marriages. To a nunnery, go.

Exit HAMLET *stage right.*

OPHELIA

> O, what a noble mind is here o'erthrown!
> I see that noble and most sovereign reason,
> Like sweet bells jangled, out of tune and harsh;
> O, woe is me, to have seen what I have seen,
> > see what I see!

Exit OPHELIA *stage left.*

✳ SCENE 6. (ACT III, SCENE II)

A hall in the castle.

Enter HAMLET *and* HORATIO *from stage right.*

HAMLET
> Horatio, there is a play to-night before the king;
> One scene of it comes near the circumstance
> Which I have told thee of my father's death:
> Give him heedful note;
> For I mine eyes will rivet to his face,
> And after we will both our judgments join
> In censure of his seeming.

HORATIO
> Well, my lord.

HAMLET
> They are coming to the play; I must be idle:
> Get you a place.

SOUND OPERATOR *plays* Sound Cue #2 ("Danish march with flourish").

Enter KING CLAUDIUS, QUEEN GERTRUDE, POLONIUS, *and* OPHELIA *from stage left. Both* POLONIUS *and* OPHELIA *carry chairs.*

QUEEN GERTRUDE
> Come hither, my dear Hamlet, sit by me.

HAMLET
No, good mother, here's metal more attractive.

HAMLET sits on the floor by OPHELIA'S chair and nestles his head in her lap; she is stiff and uncomfortable, not knowing what to make of this change in HAMLET'S behavior.

SOUND OPERATOR plays Sound Cue #3 ("Dumbshow music").

The PLAYERS begin their show. Enter a king and a queen very lovingly; the queen embracing him, and he her. She bows to him. He takes her up, and declines his head upon her neck: he lies down upon a bank of flowers: she, seeing him asleep, leaves him. Anon comes in a fellow, takes off his crown, kisses it, and pours poison in the king's ears, and exit. The queen returns; finds the king dead, and mourns in anguish. The poisoner, comes in again, seeming to lament with her. The dead body stays dead. The poisoner woos the queen with gifts: she seems loath and unwilling awhile, but in the end accepts his love.

Exit PLAYERS.

OPHELIA *(to Hamlet)*
What means this, my lord?

HAMLET
It means mischief.

KING CLAUDIUS *(agitated)*
What do you call the play?

HAMLET *(stands)*
The Mouse-trap. *(dramatically)*

KING CLAUDIUS is visibly upset; he stands.

OPHELIA

The king rises.

HAMLET

What, frighted with false fire!

QUEEN GERTRUDE

How fares my lord?

KING CLAUDIUS

Give me some light: away!

ALL

Lights, lights, lights!

Exit ALL *but* HAMLET *and* HORATIO. POLONIUS *and* OPHELIA *remove their own chairs.*

HAMLET *(animated)*

O good Horatio, I'll take the ghost's word for a
thousand pound. Didst perceive?

HORATIO

Very well, my lord.

HAMLET

Upon the show of the poisoning?

HORATIO

I did very well note him.

HAMLET

I will come to my mother by and by.
Leave me, friend.

Exit HORATIO *stage left.*

'Tis now the very witching time of night,
When churchyards yawn and hell itself breathes out
Contagion to this world. Soft! Now to my mother.

Exit HAMLET *stage right.*

✳ SCENE 7. (ACT III, SCENE IV)

The Queen's closet.

Enter **NARRATOR** *from stage rear, coming downstage center.*

NARRATOR
> Hamlet confronts his mother, resulting in a bloody
> deed involving Ophelia's father, Lord Polonius; the
> Ghost returns.

Exit **NARRATOR** *stage left.*

Enter **QUEEN GERTRUDE** *and* **POLONIUS** *from stage right.*

POLONIUS
> He will come straight.
> Tell him his pranks have been too broad to bear with.
> I'll sconce me even here. *(gestures toward stage right
>   pillar)*

HAMLET *(from offstage right)*
> Mother, mother, mother!

QUEEN GERTRUDE
> Withdraw, I hear him coming.

POLONIUS *hides behind stage right pillar.*

Enter **HAMLET** *from stage left.*

HAMLET
> Now, mother, what's the matter?

QUEEN GERTRUDE
> Hamlet, thou hast thy father much offended.

HAMLET
> Mother, you have my father much offended.

QUEEN GERTRUDE
> Come, come, you answer with an idle tongue.

HAMLET
> Go, go, you question with a wicked tongue.

LORD POLONIUS *makes a coughing and rustling sound.*

HAMLET *(draws sword)*
> How now! A rat? Dead, for a ducat, dead!

HAMLET *finds* **POLONIUS** *behind the pillar and stabs him with his sword.*

LORD POLONIUS *(still hidden)*
> O!

POLONIUS *falls and dies, ending with his face away from* **HAMLET.**

QUEEN GERTRUDE
> O me, what hast thou done?

HAMLET
> Is it the king?

QUEEN GERTRUDE
> O, what a rash and bloody deed is this!

HAMLET

> Almost as bad as kill a king, and marry with his
> brother.

QUEEN GERTRUDE

> As kill a king!

HAMLET

> Ay Lady, 'twas my word.

HAMLET *turns the body over and discovers it is* POLONIUS; *he is
shocked and dismayed.*

> Thou wretched, rash, intruding fool, farewell!
> I took thee for thy better:

Enter GHOST *from stage right.*

GHOST

> Do not forget: this visitation
> Is but to whet thy almost blunted purpose.
> But, look, amazement on thy mother sits:
> > (*points to* QUEEN GERTRUDE)
> Speak to her, Hamlet.

HAMLET (*addresses* QUEEN GERTRUDE; *points to* GHOST)

> Do you see nothing there?

QUEEN GERTRUDE

> Nothing at all.

HAMLET *is in disbelief that she does not see. He goes to her side
and turns her toward* GHOST.

HAMLET

> Why, look you there!
> My father!

Exit GHOST *stage right.*

QUEEN GERTRUDE
>This the very coinage of your brain:

HAMLET *(protesting)*
>It is not madness *(kneels beside* QUEEN GERTRUDE*)*
>Confess yourself to heaven; avoid what is to come.

QUEEN GERTRUDE *(disconsolate)*
>O Hamlet, thou hast cleft my heart in twain.

HAMLET
>O, throw away the worser part of it,
>And live the purer with the other half.

Exit HAMLET *stage left.* QUEEN GERTRUDE *looks after him in horror and dismay, then exits rapidly stage left.*

✳ SCENE 8. (ACT IV, SCENE V)

Elsinore. A room in the castle.

Enter NARRATOR *from stage rear, coming downstage center.*

NARRATOR
    Tragic events have had their effect on Ophelia.

Exit NARRATOR *stage left.*

Enter QUEEN GERTRUDE *and* KING CLAUDIUS *from stage right.*
KING CLAUDIUS *sits in throne and* QUEEN GERTRUDE *sits in chair.*

Enter OPHELIA *from stage right.* QUEEN GERTRUDE *goes to greet her, but* OPHELIA *sweeps right by.*

OPHELIA
    Where is the beauteous majesty of Denmark?

QUEEN GERTRUDE
    How now, Ophelia!

OPHELIA *(singing)*
    He is dead and gone, lady,
    He is dead and gone;
    At his head a grass-green turf,
    At his heels a stone.

KING CLAUDIUS *tries to approach* OPHELIA, *but she dances away.*

KING CLAUDIUS
How do you, pretty lady?

OPHELIA (*singing*)
To-morrow is Saint Valentine's day,
All in the morning betime,
And I a maid at your window,

OPHELIA *comes too close to the standing king; he sits.*

To be your Valentine.

OPHELIA *dances in front of the king, then spins off.*

KING CLAUDIUS (*moves close to* QUEEN GERTRUDE)
How long hath she been thus?

QUEEN GERTRUDE *indicates she does not know the answer.*

OPHELIA
I cannot choose but weep, to think they should lay
him i' the cold ground. My brother shall know of it.

OPHELIA *sits in the chair and summons an invisible horse-drawn carriage.*

Come, my coach!

OPHELIA *begins to exit, skipping like a horse.*

Good night, ladies; good night, sweet ladies; good
night, good night.

Exit OPHELIA *stage right.*

KING CLAUDIUS
O, this is the poison of deep grief; it springs

All from her father's death. Poor Ophelia
Divided from herself and her fair judgment.

A noise sounds from offstage.

Enter LAERTES, *armed, from stage left. He moves behind* KING
CLAUDIUS *and puts a sword to the king's throat.*

LAERTES

Where is this king? O thou vile king.
Where is my father?

KING CLAUDIUS

Dead.

LAERTES

How came he dead? I'll not be juggled with:
To hell, allegiance! Vows, to the blackest devil!
I'll be revenged most thoroughly for my father.

LAERTES *threatens* KING CLAUDIUS *with his sword.*

KING CLAUDIUS *(stands)*

I am guiltless of your father's death,
And am most sensible in grief for it.

LAERTES

How now! What noise is that?

Re-enter OPHELIA *from stage right, disheveled and with hair
a mess.*

O heat, dry up my brains!
By heaven, thy madness shall be paid by weight.
O rose of May!
Dear maid, kind sister, sweet Ophelia!

LAERTES *goes to hold* OPHELIA'S *hand. She takes his hand, spins around, and then lets go.*

OPHELIA *(singing)*
> And will he not come again?
> And will he not come again?
> No, no, he is dead:
> Go to thy death-bed:
> He never will come again.

Exit OPHELIA *stage right.*

LAERTES
> Do you see this, O God?

KING CLAUDIUS
> Where the offense is let the great axe fall.
> I pray you, go with me.

Exit ALL *stage right.*

STAGEHANDS *set throne near chair stage left.*

✳ SCENE 9. (ACT V, SCENE II. ADDITIONAL MATERIAL FROM ACT III, SCENE I.)

A hall in the castle

Enter NARRATOR *from stage rear, coming downstage center.*

NARRATOR
> Hamlet and Laertes duel. Poison is involved. I do not predict a happy ending.

Exit NARRATOR *stage left.*

Enter HAMLET *and* HORATIO *from stage right.*

HAMLET
> There's a divinity that shapes our ends,
> Rough-hew them how we will,—

HORATIO
> That is most certain.

HAMLET
> Is't not perfect conscience,
> To quit him with this arm?

HORATIO
> Peace! Who comes here?

Enter OSRIC *from stage right.*

OSRIC
> Your lordship is right welcome back to Denmark.

HAMLET
> I humbly thank you, sir.

OSRIC
> My lord, his majesty bade me signify to you that he has laid a great wager on your head: Here is newly come to court Laertes. The king, sir, hath laid, that in a dozen passes between yourself and him, he shall not exceed you three hits.

HAMLET
> Let the foils be brought, the gentleman willing, and the king hold his purpose, I will win for him.

OSRIC
> The king and queen and all are coming down.

HORATIO
> You will lose this wager, my lord.

HAMLET
> There's a special providence in the fall of a sparrow. The readiness is all.

Enter KING CLAUDIUS, QUEEN GERTRUDE, LAERTES, OSRIC, *and* assorted LORDS. *The* LORDS *bear a table and bottles of wine.*

KING CLAUDIUS
> Come, Hamlet, come, and take this hand from me.

KING CLAUDIUS *puts* LAERTES'S *hand into* HAMLET'S.

HAMLET

Give me your pardon, sir: I've done you wrong;
I here proclaim was madness.

LAERTES

I stand aloof; and will no reconcilement.

KING CLAUDIUS

Give them the foils, young Osric.

LAERTES

This is too heavy, let me see another.

A LORD *gives the poisoned sword to* OSRIC *to give to* LAERTES.
HAMLET *and* LAERTES *prepare to duel.*

KING CLAUDIUS

The king shall drink to Hamlet's better breath;
Come, begin.

LAERTES

Come, my lord.

HAMLET *and* LAERTES *begin to duel.*

HAMLET

One.

LAERTES

No.

HAMLET

Judgment.

OSRIC

A hit, a very palpable hit.

LAERTES
>Well; again.

KING CLAUDIUS
>Stay; give me drink. Hamlet, this pearl is thine;
>Here's to thy health.

HAMLET
>I'll play this bout first; set it by awhile. Come.

HAMLET *and* LAERTES *resume the duel.*

>Another hit; what say you?

LAERTES
>A touch, a touch, I do confess.

QUEEN GERTRUDE
>The queen carouses to thy fortune, Hamlet.

HAMLET
>Good madam!

KING CLAUDIUS
>Gertrude, do not drink.

QUEEN GERTRUDE
>I will, my lord; I pray you, pardon me.

KING CLAUDIUS *(aside)*
>It is the poison'd cup: it is too late.

QUEEN GERTRUDE *offers her drink to* HAMLET.

HAMLET
>I dare not drink yet, madam; by and by.

LAERTES
>Have at you now!

LAERTES *wounds* HAMLET; *in scuffling, they change rapiers, and* HAMLET *wounds* LAERTES.

QUEEN GERTRUDE *falls.*

HORATIO
>They bleed on both sides. How is it, my lord?

OSRIC
>How is't, Laertes?

LAERTES
>I am justly kill'd with mine own treachery.

HAMLET
>How does the queen?

KING CLAUDIUS
>She swounds to see them bleed.

QUEEN GERTRUDE
>No, no, the drink, the drink,—O my dear Hamlet,—
>The drink, the drink! I am poison'd.

QUEEN GERTRUDE *dies.*

HAMLET
>O villany! Let the door be lock'd:
>Treachery! Seek it out.

LAERTES
>It is here, Hamlet: Hamlet, thou art slain;

The treacherous instrument is in thy hand, envenom'd:
Thy mother's poison'd: The king's to blame.

HAMLET

The point!—Envenom'd too!
Then, venom, to thy work.

HAMLET *stabs* KING CLAUDIUS.

KING CLAUDIUS

O, yet defend me, friends; I am but hurt.

HAMLET

Here, thou incestuous, murderous, damned Dane,
Drink off this potion. Is thy union here?
Follow my mother.

KING CLAUDIUS *dies.*

LAERTES

He is justly served;
Exchange forgiveness with me, noble Hamlet:
Mine and my father's death come not upon thee,
Nor thine on me.

LAERTES *dies.*

HAMLET

Heaven make thee free of it! I follow thee.
I am dead, Horatio. Wretched queen, adieu!
Horatio, I am dead;
Thou livest; report me and my cause aright
To the unsatisfied.
If thou didst ever hold me in thy heart
In this harsh world draw thy breath in pain,
To tell my story.

O, I die, Horatio;
The potent poison quite o'er-crows my spirit:
The rest is silence.

HAMLET *dies.*

HORATIO

Now cracks a noble heart. Good night sweet prince:
And flights of angels sing thee to thy rest!

ALL *gather onstage and begin to speak.*

ALL

To be, or not to be: that is the question:
Whether 'tis nobler in the mind to suffer
The slings and arrows of outrageous fortune,
Or to take arms against a sea of troubles,
And by opposing end them? To die: to sleep;
No more; and by a sleep to say we end
The heart-ache and the thousand natural shocks
That flesh is heir to,'tis a consummation
Devoutly to be wish'd.To die, to sleep;
To sleep: perchance to dream: ay, there's the rub;
For in that sleep of death what dreams may come
When we have shuffled off this mortal coil,
Must give us pause: there's the respect
That makes calamity of so long life;
Thus conscience does make cowards of us all;
And thus the native hue of resolution
Is sicklied o'er with the pale cast of thought,
And enterprises of great pitch and moment
With this regard their currents turn awry,
And lose the name of action!

ALL *hold hands and take a bow. Exeunt.*

✳ APPENDIX 1: DUMBSHOW

Please make this big and exaggerated, both physically and facially, and hold your poses for a second.

1 PLAYER KING *and* QUEEN *enter stately, gracefully, and arm in arm.*

2 PLAYER QUEEN *reaches her hand out, and* KING *kisses it.*

3 PLAYER QUEEN *lays her head on* KING'S *chest.*

4 KING *is contented and gives a big yawn with arms outstretched.*

5 QUEEN *makes a graceful wave toward ground as if to say, "Why don't you lie down here?"*

6 QUEEN *looks toward audience and places her hands over her heart, and gives* KING *a loving, sleepy-lidded smile toward audience.*

7 QUEEN *exits backward with small, slow steps, all the while gazing fondly at sleeping* KING, *and all the while with her hand over her heart.*

8 POISONER *sneaks on stage, tip-toeing and looking around.*

9 POISONER *spies crown, stops, freezes, and very slowly takes* KING'S *crown off his head and kisses it. Returns it gently, slowly, and nervously to* KING'S *head.*

10 POISONER *takes poison bottle out of pocket and shows it to audience with slow, evil, swooping gestures.*

11 POISONER *unscrews poison bottle.*

12 POISONER *pours poison in* KING'S *ear.*

13 KING *dies;* POISONER *looks out villainously at audience.*

14 POISONER *sneaks off looking around, tip-toeing, trying not to get caught.*

15 QUEEN *starts walking onstage gracefully, arms out, then stiffens and freezes when she sees the body, turns to audience with look of horror, hands on either side of face: "Oh no!"*

16 QUEEN *runs off stage in a panic, arms and hands up to her sides and shaking.*

17 QUEEN *re-enters, weeping, face in hands, with face directly toward audience.* POISONER *has his hand on* QUEEN'S *shoulder.*

18 QUEEN *throws self on ground, with weeping head on* KING'S *chest, facing audience.* POISONER *has his hands on the* QUEEN'S *shoulders.*

19 QUEEN *looks toward audience with her hand on her heart and a big weeping face.*

20 POISONER, *still touching* QUEEN'S *shoulders, looks out at audience with villainous, scheming face.*

21 *When* SOUND OPERATOR *sees* QUEEN *and* POISONER *facing audience, he stops the music.*

22 *As soon as music stops,* ALL ROYAL AUDIENCE *applauds.*

23 *The three* PLAYERS *quickly stand up, with* KING *in center, holding hands, lifting hands over heads, and bow to* ROYAL AUDIENCE, *then exit quickly.*

24 *In audience,* KING CLAUDIUS *is visibly upset and starts to respond.*

✳ APPENDIX 2: TO BE OR NOT TO BE SPEECH BREAKDOWN

ALL *start to gather onstage.*

ACTOR 1

To be, or not to be: that is the question:

ACTOR 2

Whether 'tis nobler in the mind to suffer
The slings and arrows of outrageous fortune,

ACTOR 3

Or to take arms against a sea of troubles,
And by opposing end them?

ALL

To die: to sleep;
No more;

ACTOR 4

and by a sleep to say we end
The heart-ache and the thousand natural shocks
That flesh is heir to,

ACTOR 5

'tis a consummation
Devoutly to be wish'd.

ALL

> To die, to sleep;

ACTOR 6

> To sleep: perchance to dream: ay, there's the rub;

ACTOR 7

> For in that sleep of death what dreams may come
> When we have shuffled off this mortal coil,

ALL

> Must give us pause:

ACTOR 8

> there's the respect
> That makes calamity of so long life;

ALL

> Thus conscience does make cowards of us all;

ACTOR 9

> And thus the native hue of resolution
> Is sicklied o'er with the pale cast of thought,

ALL

> And enterprises of great pitch and moment
> With this regard their currents turn awry,
> And lose the name of action!

ALL *hold hands, lifting arms in air, and take a big bow to thunderous applause.*

✳ PERFORMING SHAKESPEARE

BACKGROUND:
HOW *THE 30-MINUTE SHAKESPEARE* WAS BORN

In 1981 I performed a "Shakespeare Juggling" piece called "To Juggle or Not To Juggle" at the first Folger Library Secondary School Shakespeare Festival. The audience consisted of about 200 Washington, D.C. area high school students who had just performed thirty-minute versions of Shakespeare plays for each other and were jubilant over the experience. I was dressed in a jester's outfit, and my job was to entertain them. I juggled and jested and played with Shakespeare's words, notably Hamlet's "To be or not to be" soliloquy, to very enthusiastic response. I was struck by how much my "Shakespeare Juggling" resonated with a group who had just performed Shakespeare themselves. "Getting" Shakespeare is a heady feeling, especially for adolescents, and I am continually delighted at how much joy and satisfaction young people derive from performing Shakespeare. Simply reading and studying this great playwright does not even come close to inspiring the kind of enthusiasm that comes from performance.

Surprisingly, many of these students were not "actor types." A good percentage of the students performing Shakespeare that day were part of an English class which had rehearsed the plays during class time. Fifteen years later, when I first started directing plays in D.C. public schools as a Teaching Artist with the Folger Shakespeare Library, I entered a ninth grade English class as a guest and spent two or three days a week for two or three months preparing students for the Folger's annual Secondary School Shakespeare Festival. I have conducted this annual residency with the Folger ever since.

Every year for seven action-packed days, eight groups of students between grades seven and twelve tread the boards onstage at the Folger's Elizabethan Theatre, a grand recreation of a sixteenth-century venue with a three-tiered gallery, carved oak columns, and a sky-painted canopy.

As noted on the Folger website (www.folger.edu), "The festival is a celebration of the Bard, not a competition. Festival commentators—drawn from the professional theater and Shakespeare education communities—recognize exceptional performances, student directors, and good spirit amongst the students with selected awards at the end of each day. They are also available to share feedback with the students."

My annual Folger Teaching Artist engagement, directing a Shakespeare play in a public high school English class, is the most challenging and the most rewarding thing I do all year. I hope this book can bring you the same rewards.

GETTING STARTED: GAMES

How can you get an English class (or any other group of young people, or even adults) to start the seemingly daunting task of performing a Shakespeare play? You have already successfully completed the critical first step, which is buying this book. You hold in your hand a performance-ready, thirty-minute cutting of a Shakespeare play, with stage directions to get the actors moving about the stage purposefully. But it's a good idea to warm the group up with some theater games.

One good initial exercise is called "Positive/Negative Salutations." Students stand in two lines facing each other (four or five students in each line) and, reading from index cards, greet each other, first with a "Positive" salutation in Shakespeare's language (using actual phrases from the plays), followed by a "negative" greeting.

Additionally, short vocal exercises are an essential part of the preparation process. The following is a very simple and effective vocal warm-up: Beginning with the number two, have the whole group count to twenty using increments of two (i.e., "Two, four, six . . ."). Increase the volume slightly with each number, reaching top volume with "twenty," and then decrease the volume while counting back down, so that the students are practically whispering when they arrive again at "two." This exercise teaches dynamics and allows them to get loud as a group without any individual pressure. Frequently during a rehearsal period, if a student is mumbling inaudibly, I will refer back to this exercise as a reminder that we can and often do belt it out!

"Stomping Words" is a game that is very helpful at getting a handle on Shakespeare's rhythm. Choose a passage in iambic pentameter and have the group members walk around the room in a circle, stomping their feet on the second beat of each line:

Two **house**-holds, **both** a-**like** in **dig**-nity
In **fair** Ve-**rona Where** we **lay** our **scene**

Do the same thing with a prose passage, and have the students discuss their experience with it, including points at which there is an extra beat, etc., and what, if anything, it might signify.

I end every vocal warm-up with a group reading of one of the speeches from the play, emphasizing diction and projection, bouncing off consonants, and encouraging the group members to listen to each other so that they can speak the lines together in unison. For variety I will throw in some classic "tongue twisters" too, such as, "The sixth sheik's sixth sheep is sick."

The Folger Shakespeare Library's website (http://www.folger.edu) and their book series *Shakespeare Set Free,* edited by Peggy O'Brien, are two great resources for getting started with a performance-based teaching of Shakespeare in the classroom. The Folger website has numerous helpful resources and activities, many submitted by teachers, for helping a class actively participate in the process of getting to know a Shakespeare play. For more simple theater games, Viola Spolin's *Theatre Games for the Classroom* is very helpful, as is one I use frequently, *Theatre Games for Young Performers*.

HATS AND PROPS

Introducing a few hats and props early in the process is a good way to get the action going. Hats, in particular, provide a nice avenue for giving young actors a non-verbal way of getting into character. In the opening weeks, when students are still holding onto their scripts, a hat can give an actor a way to "feel" like a character. Young actors are natural masters at injecting their own personality into what they wear, and even small choices made with how a hat is worn (jauntily, shadily, cockily, mysteriously) provide a starting point for discussion of specific characters, their traits, and their relationships with other characters. All such discussions always lead back to one thing: the text. "Mining the text" is consistently the best strategy for uncovering the mystery of Shakespeare's language. That is where all the answers lie: in the words themselves.

WHAT DO THE WORDS MEAN?

It is essential that young actors know what they are saying when they recite Shakespeare. If not, they might as well be scat singing, riffing on sounds and rhythm but not conveying a specific meaning. The real question is: What do the words mean? The answer is multifaceted, and can be found in more than one place. The New Folger Library paperback editions of the plays themselves (edited by Barbara Mowat and Paul Werstine, Washington Square Press) are a great resource for understanding Shakespeare's words and passages and "translating" them into modern English. These editions also contain chapters on Shakespeare's language, his life, his theater, a "Modern Perspective," and further reading. There is a wealth of scholarship embedded in these wonderful books, and I make it a point to read them cover to cover before embarking on a play-directing project. At the very least, it is a good idea for any adult who intends to direct a Shakespeare play with a group of students to go through the explanatory notes that appear on the pages facing the text. These explanatory notes are an indispensable "translation tool."

The best way to get students to understand what Shakespeare's words mean is to ask them what they think they mean. Students have their own associations with the words and with how they sound and feel. The best ideas on how to perform Shakespeare often come directly from the students, not from anybody else's notion. If a student has an idea or feeling about a word or passage, and it resonates with her emotionally, physically, or spiritually, then Shakespeare's words can be a vehicle for her feelings. That can result in some powerful performances!

I make it my job as director to read the explanatory notes in the Folger text, but I make it clear to the students that almost "anything goes" when trying to understand Shakespeare. There are no wrong interpretations. Students have their own experiences, with some shared and some uniquely their own. If someone has an association with the phrase "canker-blossom," or if the words make that student or his character feel or act a certain way, then that is the "right" way to decipher it.

I encourage the students to refer to the Folger text's explanatory notes and to keep a pocket dictionary handy. Young actors must attach some meaning to every word or line they recite. If I feel an actor is glossing over a word, I will stop him and ask him what he is saying. If he doesn't know, we will figure it out together as a group.

PROCESS VS. PRODUCT

The process of learning Shakespeare by performing one of his plays is more important than whether everybody remembers his lines or whether somebody misses a cue or an entrance. But my Teaching Artist residencies have always had the end goal of a public performance for about 200 other students, so naturally the performance starts to take precedence over the process somewhere around Dress Rehearsal in the students' minds. It is my job to make sure the actors are prepared—otherwise they will remember the embarrassing moment of a public mistake and not the glorious triumph of owning a Shakespeare play.

In one of my earlier years of play directing, I was sitting in the audience as one of my narrators stood frozen on stage for at least a minute, trying to remember her opening line. I started scrambling in my backpack below my seat for a script, at last prompting her from the audience. Despite her fine performance, that embarrassing moment is all she remembered from the whole experience. Since then I have made sure to assign at least one person to prompt from backstage if necessary. Additionally, I inform the entire cast that if somebody is dying alone out there, it is okay to rescue him or her with an offstage prompt.

There is always a certain amount of stage fright that will accompany a performance, especially a public one for an unfamiliar audience. As a director, I live with stage fright as well, even though I am not appearing on stage. The only antidote to this is work and preparation. If a young actor is struggling with her lines, I make sure to arrange for a session where we run lines over the telephone. I try to set up a buddy system so that students can run lines with their peers, and this often works well. But if somebody does not have a "buddy," I will personally make the time to help out myself. As I assure my students from the outset, I am not going to let them fail or embarrass themselves. They need an experienced leader. And if the leader has experience in teaching but not in directing Shakespeare, then he needs this book!

It is a good idea to culminate in a public performance, as opposed to an in-class project, even if it is only for another classroom. Student actors want to show their newfound Shakespearian thespian skills to an outside group, and this goal motivates them to do a good job. In that respect, "product" is important. Another wonderful bonus to performing a play is that it is a unifying group effort. Students learn teamwork. They learn to give focus to another actor when he is speaking, and to play off of other characters. I like to end each performance with the entire cast reciting a passage in unison. This is a powerful ending, one that reaffirms the unity of the group.

SEEING SHAKESPEARE PERFORMED

It is very helpful for young actors to see Shakespeare performed by a group of professionals, whether they are appearing live on stage (preferable but not always possible) or on film. Because an entire play can take up two or more full class periods, time may be an issue. I am fortunate because thanks to a local foundation that underwrites theater education in the schools, I have been able to take my school groups to a Folger Theatre matinee of the play that they are performing. I always pick a play that is being performed locally that season. But not all group leaders are that lucky. Fortunately, there is the Internet, specifically YouTube. A quick YouTube search for "Shakespeare" can unearth thousands of results, many appropriate for the classroom.

The first "Hamlet" result showed an 18-year-old African-American actor on the streets of Camden, New Jersey, delivering a riveting performance of Hamlet's "The play's the thing." The second clip was from *Cat Head Theatre,* an animation of cats performing Hamlet. Of course, YouTube boasts not just alley cats and feline thespians, but also clips by true legends of the stage, such as John Gielgud and Richard Burton. These clips can be saved and shown in classrooms, providing useful inspiration.

One advantage of the amazing variety of clips available on YouTube is that students can witness the wide range of interpretations for any given scene, speech, or character in Shakespeare, thus freeing them from any preconceived notion that there is a "right" way to do it.

Furthermore, modern interpretations of the Bard may appeal to those who are put off by the "thees and thous" of Elizabethan speech.

By seeing Shakespeare performed either live or on film, students are able to hear the cadence, rhythm, vocal dynamics, and pronunciation of the language, and they can appreciate the life that other actors breathe into the characters. They get to see the story told dramatically, which inspires them to tell their own version.

PUTTING IT ALL TOGETHER: THE STEPS

After a few sessions of theater games to warm up the group, it's time to begin the process of casting the play. Each play cutting in *The 30-Minute Shakespeare* series includes a cast list and a sample program, demonstrating which parts have been divided. Cast size is generally between twenty and thirty students, with major roles frequently assigned to more than one performer. In other words, one student may play Juliet in the first scene, another in the second scene, and yet another in the third. This will distribute the parts evenly so that there is no "star of the show." Furthermore, this prevents actors from being burdened with too many lines. If I have an actor who is particularly talented or enthusiastic, I will give her a bigger role. It is important to go with the grain—one cast member's enthusiasm can be contagious.

I provide the performer of each shared role with a similar headpiece and/or cape, so that the audience can keep track of the characters. When there are sets of twins, I try to use blue shirts and red shirts, so that the audience has at least a fighting chance of figuring it out! Other than these costume consistencies, I rely on the text and the audience's observance to sort out the doubling of characters. Generally, the audience can follow because we are telling the story.

Some participants are shy and do not wish to speak at all on stage. To these students I assign non-speaking parts and technical roles such as sound operator and stage manager. However, I always get everybody on stage at some point, even if it is just for the final group speech, because I want every group member to experience what it is like to be on a stage as part of an ensemble.

CASTING THE PLAY

Young people can be self-conscious and nervous with "formal" auditions, especially if they have little or no acting experience.

I conduct what I call an "informal" audition process. I hand out a questionnaire asking students if there is any particular role that they desire, whether they play a musical instrument. To get a feel for them as people, I also ask them to list one or two hobbies or interests. Occasionally this will inform my casting decisions. If someone can juggle, and the play has the part of a Fool, that skill may come in handy. Dancing or martial arts abilities can also be applied to roles.

For the auditions, I do not use the cut script. I have students stand and read from the Folger edition of the complete text in order to hear how they fare with the longer passages. I encourage them to breathe and carry their vocal energy all the way to the end of a long line of text. I also urge them to play with diction, projection, modulation, and dynamics, elements of speech that we have worked on in our vocal warm-ups and theater games.

I base my casting choices largely on reading ability, vocal strength, and enthusiasm for the project. If someone has requested a particular role, I try to honor that request. I explain that even with a small part, an actor can create a vivid character that adds a lot to the play. Wide variations in personality types can be utilized: if there are two students cast as Romeo, one brooding and one effusive, I try to put the more brooding Romeo in an early lovelorn scene, and place the effusive Romeo in the balcony scene. Occasionally one gets lucky, and the doubling of characters provides a way to match personality types with different aspects of a character's personality. But also be aware of the potential serendipity of non-traditional casting. For example,

I have had one of the smallest students in the class play a powerful Othello. True power comes from within!

Generally, I have more females than males in a class, so women are more likely (and more willing) to play male characters than vice versa. Rare is the high school boy who is brave enough to play a female character, which is unfortunate because it can reap hilarious results.

GET OUTSIDE HELP

Every time there is a fight scene in one of the plays I am directing, I call on my friend Michael Tolaydo, a professional actor and theater professor at St. Mary's College, who is an expert in all aspects of theater, including fight choreography. Not only does Michael stage the fight, but he does so in a way that furthers the action of the play, highlighting character's traits and bringing out the best in the student actors. Fight choreography must be done by an expert or somebody could get hurt. In the absence of such help, super slow-motion fights are always a safe bet and can be quite effective, especially when accompanied by a soundtrack on the boom box.

During dress rehearsals I invite my friend Hilary Kacser. a Washington-area actor and dialect coach for two decades. Because I bring her in late in the rehearsal process, I have her direct her comments to me, which I then filter and relay to the cast. This avoids confusing the cast with a second set of directions. This caveat only applies to general directorial comments from outside visitors. Comments on specific artistic disciplines such as dance, music, and stage combat can come from the outside experts themselves.

If you work in a school, you might have helpful resources within your own building, such as a music or dance teacher who could contribute their expertise to a scene. If nobody is available in your school, try seeking out a member of the local professional theater. Many local performing artists will be glad to help, and the students are usually thrilled to have a visit from a professional performer.

LET STUDENTS BRING THEMSELVES INTO THE PLAY

The best ideas often come from the students themselves. If a young actor has a notion of how to play a scene, I will always give that idea a try. In a rehearsal of *Henry IV, Part 1*, one traveler jumped into the other's arms when they were robbed. It got a huge laugh. This was something that they did on instinct. We kept that bit for the performance, and it worked wonderfully.

As a director, you have to foster an environment in which that kind of spontaneity can occur. The students have to feel safe to experiment. In the same production of *Henry IV*, Falstaff and Hal invented a little fist bump "secret handshake" to use in the battle scene. The students were having fun and bringing parts of themselves into the play. Shakespeare himself would have approved. When possible I try to err on the side of fun because if the young actors are having fun, then they will commit themselves to the project. The beauty of the language, the story, the characters, and the pathos will follow.

There is a balance to be achieved here, however. In that same production of *Henry IV, Part 1*, the student who played Bardolph was having a great time with her character. She carried a leather wineskin around and offered it up to the other characters in the tavern. It was a prop with which she developed a comic relationship. At the end of our thirty-minute *Henry IV, Part 1*, I added a scene from *Henry IV, Part 2* as a coda: The new King Henry V (formerly Falstaff's drinking and carousing buddy Hal) rejects Falstaff, banishing him from within ten miles of the King. It is a sad and sobering moment, one of the most powerful in the play.

But at the performance, in the middle of the King's rejection speech (played by a female student, and her only speech), Bardolph offered her flask to King Henry and got a big laugh, thus not only upstaging the King but also undermining the seriousness and poignancy of the whole scene. She did not know any better; she was bringing herself to the character as I had been encouraging her to do. But it was inappropriate, and in subsequent seasons, if I foresaw something like that happening as an individual joyfully occupied a character, I attempted to prevent it. Some things we cannot predict. Now I make sure to issue a statement warning against changing any of the blocking on show day, and to watch out for upstaging one's peers.

FOUR FORMS OF ENGAGEMENT: VOCAL, EMOTIONAL, PHYSICAL, AND INTELLECTUAL

When directing a Shakespeare play with a group of students, I always start with the words themselves because the words have the power to engage the emotions, mind, and body. Also, I start with the words in action, as in the previously mentioned exercise, "Positive and Negative Salutations." Students become physically engaged; their bodies react to the images the words evoke. The words have the power to trigger a switch in both the teller and the listener, eliciting both an emotional and physical reaction. I have never heard a student utter the line "Fie! Fie! You counterfeit, you puppet you!" without seeing him change before my eyes. His spine stiffens, his eyes widen, and his fingers point menacingly.

Having used Shakespeare's words to engage the students emotionally and physically, one can then return to the text for a more reflective discussion of what the words mean to us personally. I always make sure to leave at least a few class periods open for discussion of the text, line by line, to ensure that students understand intellectually what they feel viscerally. The advantage to a performance-based teaching of Shakespeare is that by engaging students vocally, emotionally, and physically, it is then much easier to engage them intellectually because they are invested in the words, the characters, and the story. We always start on our feet, and later we sit and talk.

SIX ELEMENTS OF DRAMA: PLOT, CHARACTER, THEME, DICTION, MUSIC, AND SPECTACLE

Over two thousand years ago, Aristotle's *Poetics* outlined six elements of drama, in order of importance: Plot, Character, Theme, Diction, Music, and Spectacle. Because Shakespeare was foremost a playwright, it is helpful to take a brief look at these six elements as they relate to directing a Shakespeare play in the classroom.

PLOT (ACTION)

To Aristotle, plot was the most important element. One of the purposes of *The 30-Minute Shakespeare* is to provide a script that tells Shakespeare's stories, as opposed to concentrating on one scene. In a thirty-minute edit of a Shakespeare play, some plot elements are necessarily omitted. For the sake of a full understanding of the characters' relationships and motivations, it is helpful to make short plot summaries of each scene so that students are aware of their characters' arcs throughout the play. The scene descriptions in the Folger editions are sufficient to fill in the plot holes. Students can read the descriptions aloud during class time to ensure that the story is clear and that no plot elements are neglected. Additionally, there are one-page charts in the Folger editions of *Shakespeare Set Free,* indicating characters' relations graphically, with lines connecting families and factions to give students a visual representation of what can often be complex interrelationships, particularly in Shakespeare's history plays.

Young actors love action. That is why *The 30-Minute Shakespeare* includes dynamic blocking (stage direction) that allows students to tell the story in a physically dramatic fashion. Characters' movements on the stage are always motivated by the text itself.

CHARACTER

I consider myself a facilitator and a director more than an acting teacher. I want the students' understanding of their characters to spring from the text and the story. From there, I encourage them to consider how their character might talk, walk, stand, sit, eat, and drink. I also urge students to consider characters' motivations, objectives, and relationships, and I will ask pointed questions to that end during the rehearsal process. I try not to show the students how I would perform a scene, but if no ideas are forthcoming from anybody in the class, I will suggest a minimum of two possibilities for how the character might respond.

At times students may want more guidance and examples. Over thirteen years of directing plays in the classroom, I have wavered between wanting all the ideas to come from the students, and deciding that I need to be more of a "director," telling them what I would like to see them doing. It is a fine line, but in recent years I have decided that if I don't see enough dynamic action or characterization, I will step in and "direct" more. But I always make sure to leave room for students to bring themselves into the characters because their own ideas are invariably the best.

THEME (THOUGHTS, IDEAS)

In a typical English classroom, theme will be a big topic for discussion of a Shakespeare play. Using a performance-based method of teaching Shakespeare, an understanding of the play's themes develops from "mining the text" and exploring Shakespeare's words and his story. If the students understand what they are saying and how that relates to their characters and the overall story, the plays' themes will emerge clearly. We always return to the text itself. There are a number of elegant computer programs, such as www.wordle.net, that will count the number of recurring words in a passage and illustrate them graphically. For example, if the word "jealousy" comes up more than any other word in *Othello,* it will appear in a larger font. Seeing the words displayed by size in this way can offer up illuminating insights into the interaction between words in the text and the play's themes. Your computer-minded students might enjoy searching for such tidbits. There are more internet tools and websites in the Additional Resources section at the back of this book.

I cannot overstress the importance of acting out the play in understanding its themes. By embodying the roles of Othello and Iago and reciting their words, students do not simply comprehend the themes intellectually, but understand them kinesthetically, physically, and emotionally. They are essentially **living** the characters' jealousy, pride, and feelings about race. The themes of appearance vs. reality, good vs. evil, honesty, misrepresentation, and self-knowledge (or lack thereof) become physically felt as well as intellectually understood. Performing Shakespeare delivers a richer understanding than that which comes from just reading the play. Students can now relate the characters' conflicts to their own struggles.

DICTION (LANGUAGE)

If I had to cite one thing I would like my actors to take from their experience of performing a play by William Shakespeare, it is an appreciation and understanding of the beauty of Shakespeare's language. The language is where it all begins and ends. Shakespeare's stories are dramatic, his characters are rich and complex, and his settings are exotic and fascinating, but it is through his language that these all achieve their richness. This leads me to spend more time on language than on any other element of the performance.

Starting with daily vocal warm-ups, many of them using parts of the script or other Shakespearean passages, I consistently emphasize the importance of the words. Young actors often lack experience in speaking clearly and projecting their voices outward, so in addition to comprehension, I emphasize projection, diction, breathing, pacing, dynamics, coloring of words, and vocal energy. *Theatre Games for Young Performers* contains many effective vocal exercises, as does the Folger's *Shakespeare Set Free* series. Consistent emphasis on all aspects of Shakespeare's language, especially on how to speak it effectively, is the most important element to any Shakespeare performance with a young cast.

MUSIC

A little music can go a long way in setting a mood for a thirty-minute Shakespeare play. I usually open the show with a short passage of music to set the tone. Thirty seconds of music played on a boom box operated by a student can provide a nice introduction to the play, create an atmosphere for the audience, and give the actors a sense of place and feeling.

iTunes is a good starting point for choosing your music. Typing in "Shakespeare" or "Hamlet" or "jealousy" (if you are going for a theme) will result in an excellent selection of aural performance enhancers at the very reasonable price of ninety-nine cents each (or free of charge, see Additional Resources section.) Likewise, fight sounds, foreboding sounds, weather sounds (rain, thunder), trumpet sounds, etc. are all readily available online at affordable cost. I typically include three sound cues in a play, just enough to enhance but not overpower a production. The boom box operator sits on the far right or left of the stage, not backstage, so he can see the action. This also has the added benefit of having somebody out there with a script, capable of prompting in a pinch.

SPECTACLE

Aristotle considered spectacle the least important aspect of drama. Students tend to be surprised at this since we are used to being bombarded with production values on TV and video, often at the expense of substance. In my early days of putting on student productions, I would find myself hamstrung by my own ambitions in the realm of scenic design.

A simple bench or two chairs set on the stage are sufficient. The sense of "place" can be achieved through language and acting. Simple set dressing, a few key props, and some tasteful, emblematic costume pieces will go a long way toward providing all the "spectacle" you need.

In the stage directions to the plays in *The 30-Minute Shakespeare* series, I make frequent use of two large pillars stage left and right at the Folger Shakespeare Library's Elizabethan Theatre. I also have characters frequently entering and exiting from "stage rear." Your stage will have a different layout. Take a good look at the performing space you will be using and see if there are any elements that can be incorporated into your own stage directions. Is there a balcony? Can characters enter from the audience? (Make sure that they can get there from backstage, unless you want them waiting in the lobby until their entrance, which may be impractical.) If possible, make sure to rehearse in that space a few times to fix any technical issues and perhaps discover a few fun staging variations that will add pizzazz and dynamics to your own show.

The real spectacle is in the telling of the tale. Wooden swords are handy for characters that need them. Students should be warned at the outset that playing with swords outside of the scene is verboten. Letters, moneybags, and handkerchiefs should all have plentiful duplicates kept in a small prop box, as well as with a stage manager, because they tend to disappear in the hands of adolescents. After every rehearsal and performance, I recommend you personally sweep the rehearsal or performance area immediately for stray props. It is amazing what gets left behind.

Ultimately, the performances are about language and human drama, not set pieces, props, and special effects. Fake blood, glitter, glass, and liquids have no place on the stage; they are a recipe for disaster, or, at the very least, a big mess. On the other hand, the props that are employed can often be used effectively to convey character, as in Bardolph's aforementioned relationship with his wineskin.

PITFALLS AND SOLUTIONS

Putting on a play in a high school classroom is not easy. There are problems with enthusiasm, attitude, attention, and line memorization, to name a few. As anybody who has directed a play will tell you, it is always darkest before the dawn. My experience is that after one or two days of utter despair just before the play goes up, show day breaks and the play miraculously shines. To quote a recurring gag in one of my favorite movies, *Shakespeare in Love:* "It's a mystery."

ENTHUSIASM, FRUSTRATION, AND DISCIPLINE

Bring the enthusiasm yourself. Feed on the energy of the eager students, and others will pick up on that. Keep focused on the task at hand. Arrive prepared. Enthusiasm comes as you make headway. Ultimately, it helps to remind the students that a "play" is fun. I try to focus on the positive attributes of the students, rather than the ones that drive me crazy. This is easier said than done, but it is important. One season, I yelled at the group two days in a row. On day two of yelling, they tuned me out, and it took me a while to win them back. I learned my lesson; since then I've tried not to raise my voice out of anger or frustration. As I grow older and more mature, it is important for me to lead by example. It has been years since I yelled at a student group. If I am disappointed in their work or their behavior, I will express my disenchantment in words, speaking from the heart as somebody who cares about them and cares about our performance and our experience together. I find that fundamentally, young people want to please, to do well, and to be liked. If there is a serious discipline problem, I will hand it over to the regular classroom teacher, the administrator, or the parent.

LINE MEMORIZATION

Students may have a hard time memorizing lines. In these cases, see if you can pair them up with a "buddy" and existing friend who will run lines with them in person or over the phone after school. If students do not have such a "buddy," I volunteer to run lines with them myself. If serious line memorization problems arise that cannot be solved through work, then two students can switch parts if it is early enough in the rehearsal process. For doubled roles, the scene with fewer lines can go to the actor who is having memorization problems. Additionally, a few passages or lines can be cut. Again, it is important to address these issues early. Later cuts become more problematic as other actors have already memorized their cues. I have had to do late cuts about twice in thirteen years. While they have gotten us out of jams, it is best to assess early whether a student will have line memorization problems, and deal with the problem sooner rather than later.

In production, always keep several copies of the script backstage, as well as cheat sheets indicating cues, entrances, and scene changes. Make a prop list, indicating props for each scene, as well as props that are the responsibility of individual actors. Direct the Stage Manager and an Assistant Stage Manager to keep track of these items, and on show days, personally double-check if you can.

In thirteen years of preparing an inner-city public high school English class for a public performance on a field trip to the Folger Secondary School Shakespeare Festival, my groups and I have been beset by illness, emotional turmoil, discipline problems, stage fright, adolescent angst, midlife crises (not theirs), and all manner of other emergencies, including acts of God and nature. Despite the difficulties and challenges inherent in putting on a Shakespeare play with a group of young people, one amazing fact stands out in my experience. Here is how many times a student has been absent for show day: Zero. Somehow, everybody has always made it to the show, and the show has gone on. How can this be? It's a mystery.

✳ PERFORMANCE NOTES: *HAMLET*

I directed this performance of *Hamlet* in 2010 with a group of high school seniors. These notes are the result of my own review of the performance video. They are not intended to be the "definitive" performance notes for all productions of *Hamlet*. Your production will be unique to you and your cast. That is the magic of live theater. What is interesting about these notes is that many of the performance details I mention were not part of the original stage directions. They either emerged spontaneously on performance day or were developed by students in rehearsal after the stage directions had been written into the script. Some of these pieces of stage business might work like a charm. Others may fall flat. My favorites are the ones that arise directly from the students themselves and demonstrate a union between actor and character, as if that individual has become a vehicle for the character he is playing. To witness an eighteen-year-old young man "become" Hamlet as Shakespeare's words leave his mouth is a memorable moment indeed.

SCENE 1 (ACT I, SCENE II)

I always enjoy picking the opening music because it is so effective in setting the mood for the scene and the play as a whole. The first sounds we hear are reminiscent of the screeching of a metal gate, along with low gong sounds. The narrator walks out slowly, looking from side to side apprehensively. By placing his hand up to the side of his face as if sharing a secret on the line, "And then there is the matter of the ghost," the narrator brings the audience into the mystery. In this way, the narrator becomes not just a purveyor of information, but a confidante. Simple physical actions go a long way toward fleshing out even the smallest roles.

On the other hand, physical actions can also be overdone. The actress playing Hamlet in Scene 1 of our production had wonderful presence, diction, commitment, and emotional delivery, but she tended to "saw the air too much" with her hands (an acting tic that Hamlet decries in his advice to the players). I appreciated her instincts toward physicalization, especially since most young actors move too little, but we had to choose specific moments where her arm movements enhanced the text rather than distracted from it. As with many scenes, by simply breaking the speech down moment-by-moment, we were able to "suit the action to the word, the word to the action."

Hamlet should be standing far stage right in this scene, apart from the other characters, moving center stage only after the others have exited. Staging in this early part of the scene should reflect Hamlet's state of mind, i.e., isolated. When Horatio enters, Hamlet perks up visibly. In fact my two twelfth grade actors devised a special handshake between Hamlet and Horatio, including a little dance step at the end, which went a long way toward illustrating their friendship. The actors devised this move themselves, and as a result, it came off as genuine. It made Hamlet and Horatio real people with a true friendship.

As Horatio explains the circumstances of the Ghost's visitation to Hamlet, Marcellus, Bernardo, and the Ghost act out the moment silently behind them. These living tableaux provide visual reinforcement for key plot elements and allow the audience to see what happened in an omitted scene. This technique is often very helpful at the beginning of the play, and can be employed during the narrator's introduction to acquaint the audience with key characters and plot elements. Audiences are not nearly as familiar with the story as the actors are. One should not assume the crowd knows the plot. Tell the tale, but also show the story in living color!

SCENE 2 (ACT I, SCENE IV)

Hamlet's first line in this scene references the cold air, so he and Horatio must shiver against the frigid weather. Shakespeare's characters use their words to describe the settings, the relationships, their thoughts and feelings, and the tale itself. It is our job to bring the words to life, and simple physical choices such as actors bracing against the cold are essential to the tale telling. When the Ghost appears, Hamlet and Horatio huddle together, not for warmth but to use each other as protection against the apparition.

The Ghost should move slowly and deliberately, economizing movement. Like the young woman playing Hamlet, the actress portraying the Ghost tended to have "happy arms," i.e., she used her sword too readily to punctuate her speech. Curtailing excessive movement in actors can be achieved by asking them to move only when there is a motivation based in the text. For example, Horatio exclaims, "It beckons you to go away with it," so clearly the ghost can beckon with his sword prior to that line. The only other movement the Ghost should make in this scene is to exit slowly after he beckons Hamlet to follow. The Ghost is not human, and his sparse and slow gestures should reflect that. In this case, stillness is more compelling and frightening than movement.

SCENE 3 (ACT I, SCENE V)

The Ghost's speeches in this scene are full of rich imagery. I asked the actress playing the Ghost to focus on the words themselves, how they sounded, and what they evoked. When an actor breaks a speech down to its individual words, she can "color" each expression and paint a beautifully textured scene for the listener. A player must appreciate the sound and feeling of the words as they leave her mouth: "father's," "spirit," "doom'd," "term," "walk," "night," "day," "confined," "fast," "fires," "foul," "crimes," "nature," "burnt," "purged," and "love." Each of these words alone is expressive, and when spoken as part of a line of Shakespeare, they are poetical.

How does one speak "poetically"? The first rule is not to rush the phrases. Many young actors hurry their lines, which perplexes the audience. Writing down beats and breathing points in the script helps curb this problem. Have the actors mark a slash in their text at appropriate breathing points. They can also underline words or syllables that are accentuated, and then experiment with changing the emphasis to hear how this changes a line's meaning.

Actors can practice "coloring" their words. Think of the word as not just a word, but also an emotion evoker. See if the word can become a poem in itself, with a richness that echoes its sentiment or enhances the image it arouses. Marking beats and coloring words will encourage actors to slow down their speech. Through her evocative expression of the Ghost's speeches, the young woman playing this tormented spirit succeeded in conveying the human emotion and beauty of the Ghost's anguish, and won an award for her efforts.

After the Ghost yells, "Swear!" from offstage, Hamlet and Horatio face each other holding hands, and bow their heads together. Brief moments like this speak volumes about the characters' relationships. Hamlet may have few true friends in the world, but he has one in Horatio. Particularly in a tragedy about a very lonely man, an intimate human stage interaction such as this can have a particular emotional resonance. Just as comedy flourishes best with a backdrop of sorrow, so the audience can feel these tender moments deeply, since they are few and far between in Hamlet's world.

SCENE 4 (ACT II, SCENE II)

This very short scene consists only of one speech by Hamlet. Its purpose is to set up "The Mousetrap," the play-within-a-play. Hamlet enters pacing while talking to himself. One can almost see the thoughts forming in his head. The actor who played Hamlet in this scene makes an interesting choice. Right before the line, "The play's the thing," he looks out at the audience and smiles, as if the idea of catching the king's conscience is bringing him pleasure.

He could have played it with intensity, anger, amazement, or any other number of emotions—but he chose joy. Many of the decisions actors make can spring directly from the text, and I encourage performers to mine the text for clues to help them in their choices. However, the writing itself does not inform all acting choices. In fact, certain acting choices inform the narrative, i.e., they enable actors and audience to view the story in a different light, based on a performance choice an actor makes. That is why it is so helpful to experiment with different interpretations of a scene before making a final choice on how to perform it.

SCENE 5 (ACT III, SCENE I)

This is a powerful and emotional scene. It is also tricky to act, because the characters' emotions, especially Hamlet's, change rapidly and unpredictably. Hamlet may be acting insane on purpose, a point that the actor and the group can explore in rehearsal. He is certainly rash and emotional. He also says some very cruel words to Ophelia, whom he once loved, according to Hamlet himself. From a staging perspective, I am interested in having the actors' physical movements reflect their emotions. Hamlet could get physical with Ophelia by holding her shoulders and pushing her, which would certainly give her something to get upset about. On the other hand, his words are more hurtful than any shove. For example, Hamlet and Ophelia approach each other until they are almost touching, and then Hamlet turns away on the line, "I love you not."

As Hamlet is exiting, he turns back to Ophelia and walks toward her for the line, "God has given you one face and you make yourselves another." This back-and-forth staging works on two levels: It reinforces the attraction/repulsion dynamic between Hamlet and Ophelia. Also, if Hamlet is indeed pretending to be mad, it paints a convincing portrait of someone who is behaving erratically. Finally on Hamlet's line, "It hath made me mad," Ophelia turns her back on him, as if it is too painful for her to see him this way.

Young actors frequently do not know what to do with their bodies while they are on stage. They either move too much or too little. Just as we can vocally color words through inflection, tone, pauses, pitch, etc. so can we add body movements that add to a word's meaning. On his line, "marry a fool," Hamlet performs a little stutter-step and a hand pose to signify a fool's jest. When Ophelia describes Hamlet's "noble and most sovereign reason, like sweet bells jangled," she lifts her arm up and rings an imaginary bell. Often a simple physical gesture can help an actor put her stamp on a character and make Shakespeare's words her own.

SCENE 6 (ACT III, SCENE II)

This scene features the Dumbshow, or "The Moustrap," whereby the traveling players act out the murder of the king via poisoning, according to Hamlet's instructions. The stage is split horizontally, with the audience (consisting of King Claudius, Queen Gertrude, Hamlet, Ophelia, and Polonius) seated stage left. Traveling players enter from stage right but play directly out to the audience for greatest visibility. The entire Dumbshow should be performed to music with a mysterious, vaguely foreboding feeling to it. I tend to choose production music myself for two reasons: first, because I have access to a large collection, and second, because I enjoy it! I consider choosing the play's music a perk of being the director, but that is simply my preference. You may have a student who is interested in sound design. If that is case, by all means assign that job to the student.

Movements during the Dumbshow should be stylized. Each pose must be held long enough for it to become a mini-tableau. For example, the poisoner should not simply enter and immediately poison the king. Rather, the whole sequence should be performed in distinct steps. Write these steps out, so the cast can see each individual move distinctly. (See Appendix 1 for a written Dumbshow sequence.) In our production, the poisoner added his own physical punctuation to the show. At the end of the Dumbshow, when he placed his hand on the player queen's shoulder (to indicate that he was entering into a relationship with her), he turned toward the audience, smiled, and gave a big wink, holding that expression while the audience laughed.

Technically, the Dumbshow is not a comedy, but it is not an inappropriate place for audience laughter. If an actor has a chance to get a laugh, that opportunity must be seized! Especially in a tragedy, moments of comic relief are important. They allow the audience to breathe, decompress a bit, and continue to be purged of pity and fear.

King Claudius can choose to respond to the traveling player's reenactment of his crime by looking horrified or standing quickly and holding his chest. Our production's Claudius chose instead to stand and slowly walk offstage, remaining nearly expressionless throughout. It was an interesting choice. By hiding his true emotions of shock and horror behind a stony stare, he indicated by omission what another actor might have chosen to depict through histrionics. I am continually fascinated by the craft of acting, and I do not profess to be an expert. In every production, I learn more from the student actors about the limitless possibilities of portraying Shakespeare's characters.

The young man playing Hamlet moves the tragedy inexorably forward, as he faces the audience directly and recites these chilling lines with diction, projection, conviction, and passion:

"'Tis now the very witching time of night,
When churchyards yawn and hell itself breathes out
Contagion to this world: Soft! Now to my mother."

By embracing the poetry and power of Shakespeare's words, this young actor makes it clear that we are now deeply involved in a story that is anything but ordinary.

SCENE 7 (ACT III, SCENE IV)

The narrator can become a character in this scene by looking around anxiously before reciting, "The Ghost returns." Having the narrator react physically to the circumstances he describes helps us to create an overall atmosphere and incorporates the narrator into the world of the play that the other actors inhabit. If everybody in the play lives in the world they create, the audience will inhabit that same domain.

Hamlet kills Polonius in this scene. In my experience, death scenes in high school productions can result in unexpected laughter. For the horror of this scene to work correctly, Polonius must fall to the floor facing away from Hamlet, with his face toward the audience and Hamlet upstage of Polonius. This way the audience can see Polonius's face, but there is a moment in which Hamlet still thinks he has killed King Claudius. As Hamlet turns Polonius on his back and recognizes him, Hamlet's face can show the growing recognition of his error.

I encourage actors not to play death scenes too casually. We may rehearse the scenes many times, but in the world of the play, this is the only time the character dies, and it should be horrifying. As with Claudius's poker face following "The Mousetrap," Hamlet can choose whether to exaggerate his facial expression into one of horror and disbelief or to experiment with other responses such as fear, sadness, numbness, etc. The important thing is for the actors to put themselves in the theatrical moment as if for the first time.

The performers in this production of *Hamlet* continually surprised me with their choices. When Queen Gertrude said, "Hamlet, thou hast thy father much offended," she wagged her fan at him as if she were scolding him. Throughout the scene, even when Hamlet was cowering and pointing at a ghost that she did not see, she continued to act the no-nonsense, practical mother, shaking her fan at him and explaining unsentimentally, "This is the very coinage of your brain." Despite her straightforward demeanor, the actress playing Gertrude then displayed a great sadness and vulnerability when she uttered, "Oh Hamlet, thou hast cleft my heart in twain." By revealing more than one facet to a character's personality, players can portray not just a character but also a complex person, in this case a practical mother whose son's rash words and deeds are breaking her heart.

SCENE 8 (ACT IV, SCENE V)

Ophelia's behavior in this scene is disturbing. Unlike Hamlet, who retains lucidity even in his "mad" moments, Ophelia's psyche has turned a corner, and she is a completely different person from the Ophelia we last saw. She sings, twirls suggestively before Claudius, stops, sings again, and then spins off. As she exits, she pantomimes as if she is riding a horse-drawn carriage. Although the actress playing Ophelia portrays her as quite mad indeed, she chooses to have a moment in the scene where the madness appears to lift briefly, leaving in its place raw emotion. After the line, "I cannot choose but weep, to think they should lay him / i' the cold ground," Ophelia stops moving, sits down, and buries her head in her hands, weeping uncontrollably. Then, just as quickly she stands and exclaims firmly, "My brother shall know of it." This powerful moment of vulnerable sorrow gives the audience a chance to experience the pain behind Ophelia's losses.

SCENE 9 (ACT V, SCENE II. ADDITIONAL MATERIAL FROM ACT III, SCENE I)

The narrator comes onstage for the final time to tell the audience what is about to transpire, and adds, "I do not predict a happy ending." This gives the spectators a chance to let out a brief laugh before the tragedy comes to a close.

This is a fairly elaborate concluding scene, featuring sword fighting, poisoning, and multiple deaths. Thanks to the assistance of my annual fight choreography resource, Michael Tolaydo, this production ends on a strong note with the climactic fight between Hamlet and Laertes. I am always grateful to have the help of a seasoned professional in matters where I lack experience and expertise. I urge anyone who is putting on a Shakespeare show with young people to seek out qualified helpers in areas such as voice, dance, music, and combat from your own circle of colleagues. We adults tend to work independently, which is handy, but only up to a point. There are people nearby who will gladly offer their talents. As an added benefit, it expands your personal and professional network. Sometimes it takes a village to build a Shakespeare play.

No production of *Hamlet* would be complete without the "To be or not to be" speech, one of the most famous soliloquies in the English language, and to my ears, one of the most beautiful. In this staging, the cast shares in the recitation. As characters enter (or rise from the ground if the character has died), each player recites one line of the speech, punctuated by phrases recited by the ensemble as a whole (see Appendix 2). Finally, all recite the final lines in unison, their voices rising to a near shout as they conclude the tragedy:

"And enterprises of great pitch and moment
With this regard their currents turn awry,
And lose the name of action!"

On the word "action" all raise their arms in the air and bow simultaneously, holding hands as a group.

Live theater is magical. It is the most dynamic form of entertainment available to us. There is nothing like the interchange between actors and audience, that vibrant energy that is created in the theatre. *Hamlet* is surely one of the most powerful and enduring dramas ever written, and we are fortunate to be able to continue giving it life, especially with young performers who can give it the vitality it deserves.

✳ *HAMLET:*
SET AND PROP LIST

SET PIECES:

Throne
Chair
Table

PROPS:

THROUGHOUT:

Swords

SCENE 2:

Armor helmet for the Ghost

SCENE 5:

Box (or bundle) of letters for Ophelia

SCENE 6:

Crown for Player King
Vial of poison for Player Poisoner

SCENE 9:

Two bottles of wine
Two goblets
Vial of poison for Laertes's sword

BENJAMIN BANNEKER ACADEMIC HIGH SCHOOL *presents*

Hamlet

By William Shakespeare

Folger Secondary School Shakespeare Festival

Tuesday, March 9th, 2010

Senior English Class | Instructor: Mr. Leo Bowman | Guest Director: Mr. Nick Newlin

Fight Choreography: Michael Tolaydo

CAST OF CHARACTERS:

Scene 1 A room of state in the castle

Narrator: Brandon Scott

King Claudius: Gabriel Massalley

Queen Gertrude: Nicolette Johnson

Polonius: Janay Wood

Laertes: Latoya Corum

Hamlet: Lorynn Holloway

Horatio: Emmanuel Eboweme

Scene 2 The platform

Narrator: Latoya Corum

Hamlet: Lorynn Holloway

Horatio: Courtney Jordan

Scene 3 Another part of the platform

Hamlet: Lorynn Holloway

Horatio: Courtney Jordan

Ghost: Brenda Reyes

Scene 4 A room in the castle

Narrator: Oluwatobi Orekunren

Hamlet: Michael T. Daniels

Scene 5 A room in the castle

Hamlet: Michasel T. Daniels

Ophelia: Brittany Whitby

Horatio: Courtney Jordan

Scene 6 A hall in the castle

Hamlet: Michasel T. Daniels

Ophelia: Brittany Whitby

Polonius: Janay Wood

Horatio: Manisha Brooks (Nish)

Queen Gertrude: Rinita Hutchinson

King Claudius: Alvin Jones

Dumb Show:

Player King: Emmanuel Eboweme

Player Queen: Nhu-Thuy Ton

Poisoner: Khaalil Akeem

Player Queen's Friend: Kyna Uwaeme

Scene 7 The Queen's room

Narrator: Courtney Jordan

Hamlet: Brandon Scott

Queen Gertrude: Nicolette Johnson

Polonius: Janay Wood

Ghost: Brenda Reyes

Scene 8 A room in the castle

Narrator: Rinita Hutchinson

Queen Gertrude: Kyna Uwaeme

King Claudius: Darrius Wade

Ophelia: Shanise Bush

Laertes: Latoya Corum

Scene 9 A hall in the castle

Narrator: Shanise Bush

Hamlet: Michael T. Daniels

Horatio: Emmanuel Eboweme

Osric: Alexander Baker

King Claudius: Oluwatobi Orekunren

Queen Gertrude: Charminika Kirkpatrick

Laertes: Jerod Hairston

Attendants: Khaalil Akeem, Brandon Scott

Stage Manager: Manisha Brooks

Boombox: Darrius Wade

There's a special providence in
the fall of a sparrow . . . The readiness is all.

Hamlet

ADDITIONAL RESOURCES

SHAKESPEARE

Shakespeare Set Free: Teaching Romeo and Juliet, Macbeth and a Midsummer Night's Dream
Peggy O'Brien, Ed., Teaching Shakespeare Institute
Washington Square Press
New York, 1993

Shakespeare Set Free: Teaching Hamlet and Henry IV, Part 1
Peggy O'Brien, Ed., Teaching Shakespeare Institute
Washington Square Press
New York, 1994

Shakespeare Set Free: Teaching Twelfth Night and Othello
Peggy O'Brien, Ed., Teaching Shakespeare Institute
Washington Square Press
New York, 1995

The *Shakespeare Set Free* series is an invaluable resource with lesson plans, activites, handouts, and excellent suggestions for rehearsing and performing Shakespeare plays in a classroom setting.

ShakesFear and How to Cure It!
Ralph Alan Cohen
Prestwick House, Inc.
Delaware, 2006

The Friendly Shakespeare: A Thoroughly Painless Guide to the Best of the Bard
Norrie Epstein
Penguin Books
New York, 1994

Brush Up Your Shakespeare!
Michael Macrone
Cader Books
New York, 1990

Shakespeare's Insults: Educating Your Wit
Wayne F. Hill and Cynthia J. Ottchen
Three Rivers Press
New York, 1991

Practical Approaches to Teaching Shakespeare
Peter Reynolds
Oxford University Press
New York, 1991

Scenes From Shakespeare:
A Workbook for Actors
Robin J. Holt
McFarland and Co.
London, 1988

101 Theatre Games for Drama
Teachers, Classroom Teachers
& Directors
Mila Johansen
Players Press Inc.
California, 1994

THEATER AND PERFORMANCE

Impro: Improvisation and the Theatre
Keith Johnstone
Routledge Books
London, 1982

A Dictionary of Theatre Anthropology:
The Secret Art of the Performer
Eugenio Barba and Nicola Savarese
Routledge
London, 1991

THEATER GAMES

Theatre Games for Young Performers
Maria C. Novelly
Meriwether Publishing
Colorado, 1990

Improvisation for the Theater
Viola Spolin
Northwestern University Press
Illinois, 1983

Theater Games for Rehearsal:
A Director's Handbook
Viola Spolin
Northwestern University Press
Illinois, 1985

PLAY DIRECTING

Theater and the Adolescent Actor:
Building a Successful School Program
Camille L. Poisson
Archon Books
Connecticut, 1994

Directing for the Theatre
W. David Sievers
Wm. C. Brown, Co.
Iowa, 1965

The Director's Vision: Play Direction
from Analysis to Production
Louis E. Catron
Mayfield Publishing Co.
California, 1989

INTERNET RESOURCES

http://www.folger.edu
The Folger Shakespeare Library's website has lesson plans, primary sources, study guides, images, workshops, programs for teachers and students, and much more. The definitive Shakespeare website for educators, historians and all lovers of the Bard.

http://www.shakespeare.mit.edu.
The Complete Works of
William Shakespeare.
All complete scripts for *The
30-Minute Shakespeare* series were
originally downloaded from this site
before editing. Links to other internet
resources.

http://www.LoMonico.com/
Shakespeare-and-Media.htm
http://shakespeare-and-media
.wikispaces.com
Michael LoMonico is Senior
Consultant on National Education
for the Folger Shakespeare Library.
His *Seminar Shakespeare 2.0* offers a
wealth of information on how to use
exciting new approaches and online
resources for teaching Shakespeare.

http://www.freesound.org.
A collaborative database of sounds
and sound effects.

http://www.wordle.net.
A program for creating "word clouds"
from the text that you provide. The
clouds give greater prominence to
words that appear more frequently in
the source text.

http://www.opensourceshakespeare
.org.
This site has good searching capacity.

http://shakespeare.palomar.edu/
default.htm
Excellent links and searches

http://shakespeare.com/
Write like Shakespeare,
Poetry Machine, tag cloud

http://www.shakespeare-online.com/

http://www.bardweb.net/

http://www.rhymezone.com/
shakespeare/
Good searchable word and phrase
finder.
Or by lines:
http://www.rhymezone.com/
shakespeare/toplines/

http://shakespeare.mcgill.ca/
Shakespeare and Performance
research team

http://www.enotes.com/william-
shakespeare

Needless to say, the internet goes on and on with valuable Shakespeare resources.
The ones listed here are excellent starting points and will set you on your way in the
great adventure that is Shakespeare.

NICK NEWLIN has been performing the comedy and variety act *Nicolo Whimsey* for international audiences for 25 years. Since 1996, he has conducted an annual play directing residency affiliated with the Folger Shakespeare Library in Washington, D.C. Newlin received a BA with Honors from Harvard University in 1982 and an MA in Theater with an emphasis in Play Directing from the University of Maryland in 1996.

THE 30-MINUTE
SHAKESPEARE

AS YOU LIKE IT 978-1-935550-06-8	**A MIDSUMMER NIGHT'S DREAM** 978-1-935550-00-6
THE COMEDY OF ERRORS 978-1-935550-08-2	**MUCH ADO ABOUT NOTHING** 978-1-935550-03-7
HAMLET 978-1-935550-24-2	**OTHELLO** 978-1-935550-10-5
HENRY IV, PAR T 1 978-1-935550-11-2	**ROMEO AND JULIET** 978-1-935550-01-3
JULIUS CAESAR 978-1-935550-29-7	**THE TAMING OF THE SHREW** 978-1-935550-33-4
KING LEAR 978-1-935550-09-9	**THE TEMPEST** 978-1-935550-28-0
LOVE'S LABOR'S LOST 978-1-935550-07-5	**TWELFTH NIGHT** 978-1-935550-04-4
MACBETH 978-1-935550-02-0	**THE TWO GENTLEMEN OF VERONA** 978-1-935550-25-9
THE MERCHANT OF VENICE 978-1-935550-32-7	**THE 30-MINUTE SHAKESPEARE ANTHOLOGY** 978-1-935550-33-4
THE MERRY WIVES OF WINDSOR 978-1-935550-05-1	

All plays $8.95, available in print and eBook editions in bookstores everywhere

"A truly fun, emotional, and sometimes magical first experience . . . guided by a sagacious, knowledgeable, and intuitive educator." —Library Journal

PHOTOCOPYING AND PERFORMANCE RIGHTS

No part of this publication may be reproduced or transmitted in any form, electronic, photocopying or otherwise, without the prior written permission of the publisher.

There is no royalty for performing *The Taming of the Shrew: The 30-Minute Shakespeare* in a classroom or on a stage; however, permission must be obtained for all playscripts used by the actors. The publisher hereby grants unlimited photocopy permission for one series of performances to all acting groups that have purchased at least five (5) copies of the paperback edition or one (1) copy of the downloadable PDF edition available for $12.95 from www.30MinuteShakespeare.com.

CPSIA information can be obtained
at www.ICGtesting.com
Printed in the USA
LVOW12s0020280317
528698LV00001B/33/P